MAKE AND CREATE
KNITTING
AND
CREATIVE
BRACELETS

Knitting projects by Sam Pyle

Published by Top That! Publishing plc
Tide Mill Way, Woodbridge, Suffolk, IP12 1AP, UK
www.topthatpublishing.com
Copyright © 2013 Top That! Publishing plc

Knitting
Getting Started

Knitting—in case you haven't figured it out yet—happens to be the coolest craft around! Even the celebs are doing it, and you know why? Once you've mastered the basics, you'll find it relaxing, creative and above all fun! Knitting is also great as you don't need loads of expensive special equipment. Most projects just need knitting or crochet needles and wool. Remember to look at the "you will need" box before each project, as this will tell you what weight and length of yarn you need. You can use any colors though!

Needle
Know-how

Did you know that everything you'll ever knit is based on the techniques that we will explain here? First, casting on—you need to do this each time you start something new. Then it's just a matter of mastering those "must-learn" stitches—knit and purl—before casting off. The following instructions apply if you are right-handed.

Casting On

1. Tie your needles together with a loose double knot, leaving a short tail. Hold the tail with your left hand and the yarn with your right. Make sure your right needle is behind the left one.

2. Pass the yarn over the point of the right-hand needle and under the left, as shown. Slide the yarn toward the pointed ends of the needles. Pull the first knot as wide as you can to make a gap.

3. Push the tip of the right-hand needle through the gap and take the yarn with it.

4. Pull the needles slightly apart. Now use the tip of the left-hand needle to lift this loop off the right-hand needle and onto the left-hand needle. You have cast your first stitch!

5. To cast on your next stitch, insert the tip of the right-hand needle into the top stitch from below and repeat steps 2–4. Keep going until you have cast on the number of stitches that you need.

Knit Stitch

1. Cast on six stitches to start.

2. Hold the needle with the cast-on stitches in your left hand. Hold the tail firmly at the back. Insert the right-hand needle from left to right through the front of the top stitch on the left-hand needle. The right needle should finish behind the left.

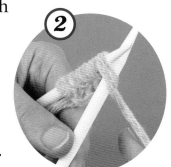

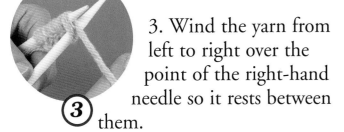

3. Wind the yarn from left to right over the point of the right-hand needle so it rests between them.

4. Pull the left-hand needle slightly back from the stitches and move the needles slightly apart to make a gap. Push the tip of the right-hand needle through the loop, bringing the yarn with it.

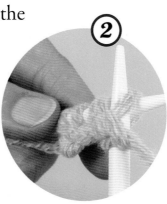

5. A new stitch should have appeared on your right-hand needle. Now "slip" your original stitch (on the left-hand needle) off its tip. To knit a row, repeat steps 2–5 until you have transferred all of the stitches from your left needle to the right. Then put your empty needle in your right hand, hold the needle with the new stitches in your left and knit another row.

Purl Stitch

1. Make a few knit stitches then bring your yarn between the needles and to the front.

2. Push the tip of the right-hand needle from right to left into the top stitch on the left-hand needle —the right needle should be above the left.

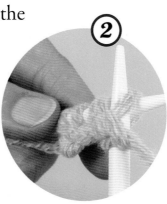

3. Now wind the yarn from right to left behind the point of the right-hand needle so that it comes between the needles.

4. Hook the yarn back and through the loop, then slip the original stitch off the tip of the left-hand needle just as you did in step 4 for the knit stitch.

5. The first purl stitch will have appeared on your right-hand needle. To keep on purling the row, repeat steps 1–4. Start by inserting the right-hand needle in front of the top stitch on the left-hand needle.

Casting Off

1. Start by knitting two stitches.

4. Keep going until you have run out of stitches on the left-hand needle and only one remains on the right-hand needle.

2. Lift the first stitch over the second and off the needle.

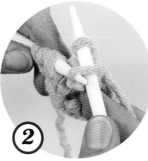

3. This leaves one stitch on the needle. Knit the next stitch as normal so that you have two stitches on the right-hand needle. Then repeat steps 2–3 all the way along the knitted row.

5. Thread the tail through the stitch then slip the stitch off the needle. Gather the yarn tightly to secure— known as "binding off."

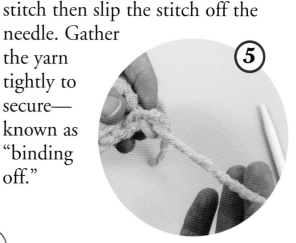

Crochet Chain

1. To crochet a chain you will need a crochet hook. Tie a loose (this is very important) knot around the top of your crochet hook, leaving a short tail, as shown.

2. Hold the hook in your right hand, then holding the tail between your thumb and first finger, bring the yarn to wrap around the tip of the hook, as shown.

3. Now bring the yarn just in front of the hooked part, as shown.

4. Pull the hook through the original loop, making sure that the part wrapped around in front stays where it is. It will take a while to get the hang of this, as the knotted loop will want to come off too! One stitch will appear above the hook, as shown.

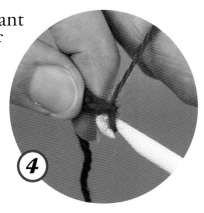

5. To make your next stitch, repeat steps 2–4 and another one will appear on the chain, as shown.

6. Repeat until you have made enough stitches to form a chain of the length you need.

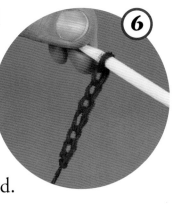

Top Tip: Keep the stitches loose by holding the last chain made between two fingers while you pull the next stitch through. If you don't, you'll have trouble working into these chains later.

Making Pompoms

1. Cut a piece of card the width you want your pompom to be. Hold the end of a ball of yarn against the card and start winding it around!

2. Keep going until the wound section is about the same width as the yarn shown in the photograph. Then carefully slide the woven section off the card.

3. Cut a long strand of yarn (around five times the width of the wound section) and tie it as tightly as you can around the middle of the woven section, as shown. Leave two tails hanging down.

4. By tying the middle, you will have created loops at either end of the wound section. Insert the tip of your scissors into one of the loops and cut through the yarn, as shown above.

5. Once you have snipped all the way through the first loop, fan out the ends, as shown. Then turn the pompom around and repeat. Shake the pompom into shape, and cut off any strands that stick out—but don't cut the tail. You'll need this to tie the pompom to your knitted project.

Cool Clutch Bag

Here you'll learn how to create a pointed edge to your knitting. This gorgeous going-out bag takes around three hours to make.

YOU WILL NEED:

- 1 skein of pure wool yarn: 3 ½ oz (100 g) / 174 yards (160 m) / no.5 bulky —must not be machine washable—very important!
- yarn needle
- ribbon 10 inches / 25 cm long
- beads
- a sewing needle

1. Cast on 30 stitches and knit 70 rows until you have a rectangular shape, as shown.

2. To make the two sloping sides of the flap, you need to knit two stitches together (we will now refer to this as "K2tog.") Insert the right needle into the first two stitches on the left needle and knit two like this. Then knit as normal to the end of the row until you have two stitches left, then "K2tog" again. Repeat until there are four stitches left, then cast off.

3. Thread your yarn needle with a spare piece of yarn and fold the bottom section up, as shown. Stitch the sides together to make an "envelope."

4. Fill a bowl with warm water and dish soap. Put your bag in and start moving it around.

5. Keep washing and rubbing until the yarn goes stiff and shrinks to a suitable bag size. Pull into shape and dry flat.

6. Sew one piece of ribbon to the point of the flap and one underneath and tie.

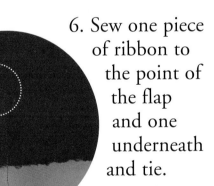

7. Then stitch on your beads to finish.

Cute 'n' Cuddly Scarf

It's all just knit, knit, knit! Put aside four hours to get a really long scarf—the pompoms can be done in minutes!

YOU WILL NEED:

- 2 skeins of "furry yarn," each one 1 ¾ oz (50 g) / 137 yards (125 m) / no.3 light DK
- yarn needle
- a strong piece of card
- scissors

1. Cast on 15 stitches. Furry yarn doesn't look much when you cast on, but it expands as you knit.

2. Start knitting! You can do as many rows as you like, just make sure it will wrap around your neck. The scarf we've started is five rows long. Once you're happy with the length, cast off.

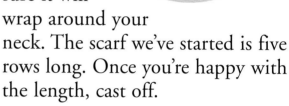

3. Thread your yarn needle with an 8 in.-long piece of furry yarn. You are now going to thread this along the width of one end of the scarf (it doesn't matter which one). Insert the needle through the knitted loops and "catch" each one.

4. Once you've threaded the yarn along the width of the scarf, gently pull each end so there's the same amount of yarn on each side.

5. Gather the scarf by pulling the threads toward each other so that the end forms a point.

6. Make a pompom (see page 7) and tie the tail to the gathered ends. Repeat steps 3–6 on the other end of the scarf to finish.

Top Tip: Some types of fluffy fun yarn knits instantly into stripes. Look for it in local craft or hobby stores.

Ribbon Pouch

No knitting, all crochet! Remember to keep your stitches nice and loose. Allow five hours to complete.

YOU WILL NEED:
- 1 skein plain or "furry" yarn 1 ¾ oz (50 g) / 66 yards (60 m) / no.4
- crochet hook
- 42 in. / 1.6 m / ribbon

1. Tie a loose loop around the hook. Hold the chain at the knot, and make a chain of two stitches (see page 6 for instructions on crocheting a chain).

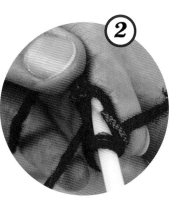

2. To make the base; put the hook into the first loop— the one with the knot.

3. Hook the yarn around, and pull through. You should have two loops left.

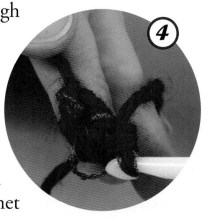

4. Hook up the yarn again and draw through both loops. You now have one loop on the hook. This is known as a single crochet stitch.

5. Repeat steps 2–3 five times. You will end up with six single crochet stitches around the original loop.

6. To complete the first round, put the hook through the first chain stitch you made.

 7. Hook the yarn and pull through the chain and original loop together. This makes a slip stitch.

8. You have completed the first round. Now make two more chains.

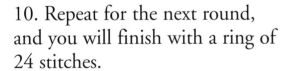 9. Then, make two single crochet stitches into each of the original six stitches. Join the first to the last by slip stitching again.

10. Repeat for the next round, and you will finish with a ring of 24 stitches.

11. For the last round, finish by crocheting one single stitch into the first, but two in the second, then one in the third, two in the fourth and alternate until you have finished a ring of 36 stitches. Slip stitch to finish. You will end up with a round base, as shown.

12. To make the sides; first, crochet a chain of three.

13. Now wrap the yarn once around the hook before you put it into the next stitch.

14. Hook up the yarn and draw it back through—you should have three loops on the hook.

15. Hook up the yarn again and draw through two loops—you should still have two loops.

16. Hook the yarn around again and draw through two loops to leave one —this is a double crochet stitch.

17. Repeat the double crochet stitches into each stitch in your base. When you get back to the start, join the first and last stitches by slip stitching into the second chain.

18. Now repeat from the chain of three to make the next row around the sides. Keep going until the sides are high enough to make a bag.

19. At the end of the last row, cut the wool 2 in. from the hook, make a slip stitch, pull the tail through the last loop and pull tight. You should have the basic nest shape.

20. Stitch the loose end down on the inside of the bag using the yarn needle.

21. Around ½ in. from the top of the bag, weave the ribbon in and out of the loose holes formed by your crocheting. Pull the ribbon gently to gather up the sides of the bag, and tie.

Top Tip: Since this project is the most intricate, we have used a plain yarn in the photos to make the steps clear. Once you're confident, you might like to use a "furry" yarn as in the finished photo on page 13!

Creative Bracelets
Getting Started

Want to show someone you care? Then why not give them a friendship bracelet!

The following pages will teach you how to make amazing friendship bracelets, simply by following the illustrated step-by-step instructions.

We've used colorful threads in the prettiest shades of blue, purple and pink to make our bracelet designs. At the beginning of each design, you'll see how much thread you need and the colors to use. You can follow our suggestions, or you can design your own color combinations using your favorite colors. Thread to make the bracelets can be bought easily and cheaply from sewing or hobby stores, where you'll be able to buy embroidery thread in all the colors of the rainbow!

Remember that you don't have to stick to threads—you can use other materials to add your own touch. Thin string and leather cord make cool, chunky-looking bracelets, while silver and gold wool can be woven through plain colors for a glittery effect. You can also add beautiful beads—simply tie them to the ends or weave them into the designs. You might want to buy a needle threader to help thread the beads.

EASY WEAVING

It's very important to keep the threads separate while you're making your bracelets. You can make an easy weaving card by using a piece of card with a bulldog clip at the top or use a clipboard.

To use a weaving card, cut the threads to the lengths in the instructions and tie them together at one end. Unless the instructions tell you differently, leave about 2 in. between the ends and the knot. Place the ends under the clip and get braiding!

BRAIDING

The simplest way of making a friendship bracelet is to braid three threads together. You do this in exactly the same way as you'd braid your hair, by crossing one strand over the other, one at a time.

ALL ABOUT KNOTS

The most important knot in the book is the basic "friendship knot." Getting the tension right is essential if you want to make successful friendship bracelets, so practice this before you start the bracelet projects.

1. Start with two pieces of thread which you have tied together. Hold thread B firmly in one hand, and pass thread A over thread B, making a loop, as shown.

2. Tuck thread A back under B, and up through the loop.

3. Pull the threads gently, so that the knot is pushed right up to the starting knot.

And that's how to tie a friendship knot!

REVERSE KNOT

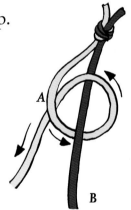

To make a reverse knot, pass thread A under thread B, then back over and down through the loop.

STARTING AND FINISHING

To tie the threads together at the start of each project, use a knot, as shown left.

Once the bracelet is long enough to go around your wrist, tie the loose ends together with the same type of knot you used at the beginning. Cut the threads, allowing an extra 2 in. after the knot.

WEARING YOUR BRACELET

Finally, use this kind of knot to tie the loose ends around your wrist.

Easy-Peasy

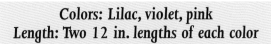

Colors: Lilac, violet, pink
Length: Two 12 in. lengths of each color

Here's a really easy-peasy design to get you started.

1. Tie the threads together with the starting knot.

2. Secure the bracelet on your weaving card. Separate the threads into pairs of the same color.

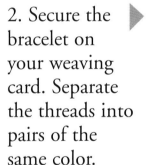

3. Bring the two lilac threads over the violet threads, so that the lilac threads are now in the middle.

4. Bring the pink threads over the lilac threads, so that pink is now in the middle.

5. Bring the violet threads over the pink threads in the same way.

6. Repeat steps 3–5, until the braid is just long enough to go around your wrist, then tie the loose ends together. Leave 2 in. and cut off any extra thread.

Why not make some really cool rings? You can use any of the bracelet designs, just braid them so they're the right length to go round your finger. Weave in a bead to make your ring look really special!

17

Two-Tone

Colors: Pale blue, black
Length: Four 15 in. lengths of each color

This checkered braid contrasts a
light and a dark color—we've used pale blue and black,
but you could use any combination of your choice.

1. Separate the threads into
two double strands of pale
blue and two double strands
of black and arrange them
on the weaving card, as
shown below.

2. Pass black threads A under black
threads B and blue threads B. Then
bring them back over blue B, as
shown. Tug the strings tightly, so that
the loop moves up to the starting knot.

3. Take blue
threads A and
pass them
under blue B
and black A,
then back
over black A.
Tug the
strings again.

4. Pull black threads B
under black threads A,
then under and over
blue A. Pull the
threads tightly.

5. Carry on until the bracelet is the right
length. After each set of steps, you should
always end up with all the blue threads on
the left, and the black threads on the right.

Flower Power

Colors: Pink, maroon
Length: Two 21 1/2 in. lengths of each color
Beads: Six gold flower beads

This pretty, delicate-looking bracelet uses two different colored threads and six gold flower beads (don't worry if you can't find these beads—others will do just as well!)

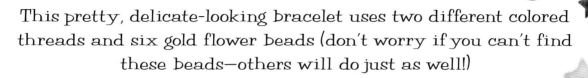

1. Tie all the threads together and separate them on the weaving card, as shown.

2. Slip one of the flower beads onto the two maroon threads, then knot all the ends together again.

3. Treating the two maroon threads as one, braid for about 1/2 in., finishing with the maroon threads in the middle, then knot the ends.

4. Thread a second bead onto the maroon threads and tie a knot.

5. Repeat steps 3 and 4, weaving three more beads into the bracelet. Braid for another 1/2 in., then finish with the last bead and a knot to tie the loose ends together.

Star Bright

Colors: Lilac, pale blue, dark blue
Length: Lilac and pale blue: one 11 in. length;
dark blue: two 11 in. lengths
Beads: Four white star beads

You'll need four white star beads to make
this star-spangled design.

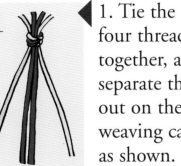 1. Tie the four threads together, and separate them out on the weaving card, as shown.

2. Take the pale blue thread over the dark blue threads, then pass it underneath the dark blue threads and return it to its original position.

3. Now take the lilac thread and do exactly the same. You'll see that you have made a cross pattern with the two different colors.

4. Repeat steps 2 and 3 for about 3/4 in., then thread one of the star beads onto the dark blue threads.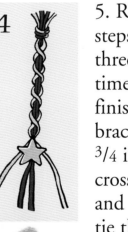

5. Repeat steps 2–4 three more times, finishing the bracelet with 3/4 in. of cross pattern and a knot to tie the loose ends together.

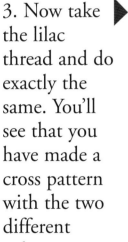

Little Twister

Colors: Purple, maroon, pale blue, lilac, dark blue, violet
Length: One 23 ½ in. length of each color
Beads: One large silver bead

This is the only bracelet that's made just by twisting!

1. Tie the threads together in a knot at one end. You won't need the weaving card for this bracelet—just tape the knot firmly to a work surface.

2. Twist all the threads tightly together in the same direction.

3. Bend the twisted threads in half, so that they twist around themselves.

4. Tie the loose ends together, then thread on a large silver bead. Tie another knot immediately after the bead. To fix your *Little Twister* around your wrist, all you have to do is pull the bead through the loop at the other end of the bracelet!

Round and Round

Colors: Purple, maroon, pale blue, lilac,
dark blue, violet, black, pink
Length: Pale blue, dark blue, purple, violet: 23 1/2 in. each;
black, pink: 19 1/2 in. each; maroon, lilac:
one 23 1/2 in. and one 19 1/2 in. length of each color
Other: Darning needle, a bead

This one's a real smoothie! As well as all your threads,
you'll also need a darning needle and a bead.

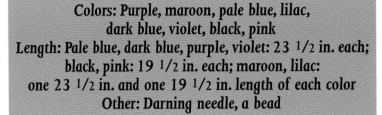

2. Thread a needle with one 50 cm length of thread. Push the needle into the bracelet about 2 cm away from the looped end, and pull the thread through. Leave a tiny piece of the loose end showing.

1. Make the *Little Twister* (page 21) using all the 23³/4 in. lengths of thread.

3. Take the thread off the needle and wind it tightly around, covering the bracelet beneath and the loose end as you go.

4. When you've nearly run out of thread,  push another color thread through the needle. Push the new thread through the bracelet, as before.

5. Start winding the new thread from the point where the previous one stopped. Cover the loose end as you go.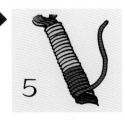

6. Carry on winding the colored threads around until you've covered the whole bracelet. Use the needle to tuck in the last loose end. Tie the bead on the end of the bracelet.

Knot Too Difficult

Colors: Maroon, dark blue
Length: Two 27 1/2 in. lengths of each color

Here's how to make a stripy bracelet using the basic friendship knot, shown on page 16. The main trick is to keep the tension nice and even as you're going along —your knots need to be tight, but not too tight. Remember, practice makes perfect!

1. Tie the ends of the threads together fairly loosely and arrange them on the weaving card, as shown.

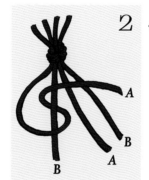

2. Take maroon A and make a friendship knot on maroon B. Hold maroon B in one hand, and tug gently while you slide the knot up the thread.

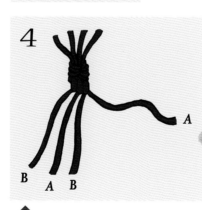

4. Now use maroon A to make two identical knots on blue A and then on blue B.

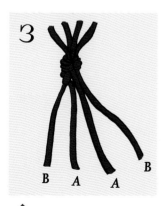

3. Make a second knot in exactly the same way. You should end up with maroon A on the right of maroon B.

(23)

5

A B A B

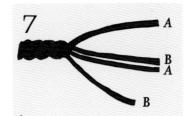

7

A
B
A
B

5. Take maroon B, and repeat steps 2–4 to make a second row of knots.

7. Finish the bracelet by braiding the threads for a further 1¹/₂ in.— just treat the middle two threads as if they were one. Knot the ends in the usual way.

6

A B A B

6. Keep making new rows, always using the thread on the outside left to make the knots.

Once you've got the general idea, you could make wider bands by using more threads. Make them all different colors, or alternate two or three stripes of color.

8. Undo the starting knot, and braid these ends for 1¹/₂ in., then knot again.

Heartstrings

Make this beautiful bracelet using the *Knot Too Difficult* design, a spare piece of thread and five blue heart beads. When you've made the basic bracelet, use a ruler to divide it into six equal parts, marking them with a felt pen, ready to sew on the heart beads.

1. Push one end of the thread through a needle and knot the other end.

2. Push the needle through the middle of the first mark on the bracelet and thread on one of the hearts.

3. Push the needle back down through the bracelet, and bring it up through the middle of the next mark, then thread on a heart. Keep doing this until you've sewn on all five hearts.

4. Finish by pushing the needle through the bracelet and tying a knot on the underside.

It's easy when you know how!